Stroll and Walk, Babble and Talk

For Mike and Sue Cleary—my first teachers
—B.P.C.

Stroll and Walk, Babble and Talk

More about Synonyms

by Brian P. Cleary

illustrations by Brian Gable

M MILLBROOK PRESS / MINNEAPOLIS

Whether you're moseying, strolling, or walking,

babbling,

chattering,

mumbling, or talking,

Synonyms help us select the right word,

MAGIC SHOW

as in sly or clever,

and say what we mean,
like superb or terrific.

Your options for words
Will quadruple—plus half—

When you start to use
all the words

that mean laugh.

Try giggle

and snicker

and chuckle and chortle—

you get to choose what works best!

You might prefer **crack up**,

and (just as a backup)

you may think that cackle has zest.

Each synonym has
quite a similar meaning,

like Washing
and Scouring,

scrubbing

and cleaning.

Synonyms sometimes will tell us degree.

Pick warm,
hot,
or steaming

When you describe tea.

They give us

alternatives,
substitutes,
choices,

and help give our stories more interesting voices!

Exit and leave,

lie and deceive,

funny and somewhat amusing.

Easy and simple,

a blemish or pimple—

just make up your mind
and start choosing!

Fast and quick,

ill and sick,

a greenback, a buck, or a dollar.

Synonyms give you selection and choice.

They make you sound just like a scholar.

So pick among difficult,
hard, or demanding.

It needn't be
frightening
or scary.

Synonyms can help you to get or procure

a mighty big vocabulary.

Now go make your writing
compelling,

exciting,

so thrilling

you might **brag** or **boast**.

So, what is a synonym?
Do you know?

Find activities, games, and more at www.brianpcleary.com

ABOUT THE AUTHOR & ILLUSTRATOR

Brian P. Cleary is the author of the Words Are CATegorical©, Math Is CATegorical©, Adventures in Memory™, and Sounds Like Reading™ series. He has also written The Laugh Stand: Adventures in Humor, Peanut Butter and Jellyfishes: A Very Silly Alphabet Book, and two poetry books. Mr. Cleary lives in Cleveland, Ohio.

BRIAN GABLE is the illustrator of several Words Are CATegorical© books, as well as the Math Is CATegorical© series. Mr. Gable also works as a political cartoonist for the Globe and Mail newspaper in Toronto, Canada.

Millbrook Press
A division of Lerner Publishing Group, Inc.
241 First Avenue North
Minneapolis, MN 55401 U.S.A.

Website address: www.lernerbooks.com

Library of Congress Cataloging-in-Publication Data

Cleary, Brian P., 1959-
    Stroll and walk, babble and talk : more about synonyms / by Brian P. Cleary ; illustrated by Brian Gable.
      p.   cm. — (Words are categorical)
    ISBN 978-0-8225-7850-5 (lib. bdg. : alk. paper)
    1. English language—Synonyms and antonyms—Juvenile literature. I. Gable, Brian, 1949- ill. II. Title.
PE1591.C554 2008
428.1—dc22   2007040360

Manufactured in the United States of America
3 — DP — 7/15/10